Curls, Kinks, and Knots of
My Dry, Thirsty, Single Soul

the 4C Heart

Curls, Kinks, and Knots of
My Dry, Thirsty, Single Soul

PARENTING FROM A WOUND

ANNA E. STYRON

Copyright © 2023 by Anna E. Styron

All rights reserved. This book or parts of it may not be reproduced in any form without permission in writing from the publisher, except that a reviewer may quote brief passages in a review.

Anna E. Styron
Garner, US
4cheartseries@gmail.com

ISBN: 978-1-7367370-5-7 (Paperback)
ISBN: 978-1-7367370-6-4 (eBook)

Library of Congress Control Number: 2023908655

Printed in the United States of America
First Edition, 2023

Cover and interior book design by Jonathan Sainsbury
Illustrations by: Jorge Leal, Instagram @george_jorge01
Copy-Edited by Abbey McLaughlin

Note to the Readers	xi
Introduction	xiii
Mamma's Love	1
I Heard a Word	5
Loving Even Judas	9
Barabbas vs. Jesus	13
Healing Waters	17
Journal Journey Entries	21
Closing Thought and Prayer	49
About the Author	55

Dedication

Jayden and Janiah, you two are the joy of my life. I pray that God blesses you both with Kingdom marriages, Kingdom children, Kingdom ministries, and Kingdom wealth to pass down to your future generations. I speak life and generational blessings over your bloodlines. I love you both so much!

To my parents, thank you for doing your best to raise us with what you knew. Now that I am a mother, I understand that as a child, we are just watching our parents grow up. Grace and mercy should be extended both ways. May we continue to grow in love, humility, and wisdom. Love you very much!

To the rest of my family and friends, thank you for your prayers and support throughout my journey. It has all meant so much to me. God bless you.

Stay healthy and wealthy in Scripture.

"That the generation to come might know them, The children who would be born, That they may arise and declare them to their children, That they may set their hope in God, And not forget the works of God, But keep His commandments."
(Psalm 78:6-7 NKJV)

Note to the Reader

Single motherhood has definitely been a journey. Motherhood itself is a journey. It is a pure reflection of who you were growing up, who you are presently, and who you are becoming. Some of us did not come from the best households, and may have an entirely different perspective of motherhood than those who come from a stable, two-parent household. Some of us may have had a two-parent household with a mother and a father who were there physically, but never really present in any other way. Many of us are wounded and scarred from our upbringings and have made internal vows never to raise our kids the way we were raised. Yet we can still find ourselves becoming the very thing we said we would never be.

Have you ever asked why that was? Why the cycle continues? Because now your children are thinking and vowing the same exact thing? And no matter how hard you try to fight it, it is a losing battle?

I was reading in Luke 8 about a demon-possessed man in the country of Gadarenes. I found it very interesting that as soon as this man saw Jesus, the demons inside of him yelled out to leave them alone (Luke 28:8 KJV). Those demons did not want the dysfunction exposed.

It was then that I came to the realization that this cycle, this dysfunction, these hurts, these wounds may be something more than a physical manifestation; perhaps a spiritual one. A lot of us grew up with our parents telling us, "What goes on in this house stays in this house." And we have ignorantly said the same thing to our children, incubating that same dysfunction. Transferring those same demons from generation to generation. Transferring those same wounds from bloodline to bloodline.

I say *no more,* women of God! It is time to renounce those internal vows, expose those demons, and cast them out in Jesus' name. The cycle ends here; it is time to heal. Healing affects speaking. We must ask ourselves: Are we speaking from our wound or from the Word? It is time to replace that pattern, that cycle, with the Word of God. Speak life into yourself and into your children, into your children's children, and to your third and fourth generations. *Amen.* May you be blessed, and your children be blessed, in Jesus' name.

> "The righteous who walks in his integrity—
> Blessed are his children after him!"
> (Proverbs 20:7 ESV)

Introduction

"So I gave my attention to the Lord God to seek
Him by prayer and supplication, with fasting,
sackcloth, and ashes." (Daniel 9:30 NASB)

So I'll just let you know now—this is not your average parenting book. We won't be discussing how to teach your kids to set a table properly or how to conduct family meetings. But we will discuss how to pick up the pieces from wherever you are, no matter what stage. From planning for a baby with your spouse, imagining one day having kids, to cooing the newborn, to managing a spunky toddler, to that curious grade-level child with all the questions, through those awkward middle-schooler years, to absent-minded teens—even to the all-knowing young adult parenting.

We are going to discuss parenting from a perspective that causes self-reflection. We are going to address *you*! You, woman of God, are the one who carries the womb to bring life into this world. But if we have not healed, been set free, or delivered from our past and present transgression, iniquities, gross injustices, or offenses, we will pass those very wounds to our future generation, and the cycle continues.

Hosea 4:6-8 says that not only are God's people destroyed for lack of knowledge, but also that He will forget our children! May that never be! As mothers, we are the caretakers, nurturers, and protectors of our children, and it is our job to make sure that God does not *forget* our children!

And how do we do that? By getting back in right standing with God ourselves by repenting of our sins, healing from the wounds of our past and present, being delivered from unholy covenants, and obeying the rules, laws, commandments, and principles laid out before us in the Word of God. By living holy, righteous, and humbly before God and others. By seeking first the Kingdom of God and all its righteousness.

Then, our children will be saved.
> *and then*, our children will be set free.
> *and then*, our children will call us blessed.
> *and then*, our relationship with our children will heal.
> *and then*, the hearts of our children will soften and return back to us.
> *and then*, your home will have order.
> *and then*, the blessing of the Lord will come upon your household.

"... *and then all these things will be added unto you.*"
(Matthew 6:33 KJV).

This is a promise from the Lord, and He does not go back on His promises. His word never returns void (Isaiah 55:11). So, women of God, it is time to de-robe these purple garments, cast off these crowns and jewels, and replace them with sackcloth and ashes because it is about to get ugly. Healing is not a pretty process. It hurts, it stings, it burns, it gets heated, there may be some swelling, some discharge, and there may be some scarring. But just know that this is all part of the process. This is what mothering is: it is *war*! You must be willing to go all in and do whatever it takes. That means killing your pride, dying to self, and rebuking your flesh. This is not for the weak or the faint of heart. And know this: Demons do not respond to *prim, proper,* or *cute*! So know how to *war,* woman of God.

Repent.
Get in His Word.

Understand Covenant.
Fast and Pray.
And, *heal* for your children and our future generation's sake.

". . . shall I give my firstborn for my transgression, The fruit of my body for the sin of my soul?" (Micah 6:7 ESV)

Mamma's Love

The love of a mother is a great joy.
The love of a mother can never let go.
It is consistent.
It is persistent.
It will never be swayed no matter what you do.
Where you go.
My prayers will always follow you.
My heart will always grow,
With more love to carry you through.
And never let you go.

—Anna E. Styron

I have heard people say parenting can be easy in some ways, hard in others. No one really gives you a road map for it—that is for sure! Hundreds of books on parenting are out there, but none really tailored to your individual circumstance. I am not even going to attempt to tell you that I have it all figured out in ten easy steps—"do it my way, guaranteed success!"—no. But I will tell you that prayer works. It is our greatest weapon. It tears down strongholds, demolishes demons, changes circumstances, and renews life. I do not know where I would be, where my children would be, nor how our lives would be if it was not for the grace of God and the open prayer line to heaven.

The parenting journey is not for the weak. It will try you and bring out some things in you that you never knew were there. Those childhood traumas that were never addressed. Those dark moments you buried growing up. Those tender wounds you tried to stitch up on your own. And now you find yourself parenting from those wounds, bleeding over your children, repeating the same hurt and trauma done to you on them. And, you do not know how to make it stop! How to fix it?! It is like you see the danger coming, but you feel helpless in preventing it.

And, now, is it too late? Is the damage done? Your kids start to see right through you. Your child calls you a hypocrite and calls you the *worst mother ever*! Your other child is torn between trying to support mom yet console their sibling. So much anger, so much rage, so much pain. It hurts. It hurts to see yourself hurting the very ones you love and gave birth to. It hurts knowing that you cannot go back to fix any of it. It hurts to come to the realization that this whole time, you have been parenting from a wound. And this wound has drained into the lives of your children. And now, not only do you have to heal, but your children do as well. And that is no small feat.

Parents are growing up too. I have told both of my children this, and my son just rolls his eyes and says jokingly that I say it so much that he is probably going to tell his kids one day. We parents are just people navigating life just as they are. They are watching us grow up, just like we are watching them—the only difference is we just have some years ahead of them. They have never been teenagers before now, and I have never been a *mother* of a teenager before now. It does not matter if you have gone through it with one child because it can be a totally new experience with your other ones. My son and daughter are complete opposites; what was an easy milestone for one was more difficult for the other. So, all that to say, give each other grace in the midst of it.

Colossians 4:21 instructs fathers not to provoke their children unless they become discouraged. Of course, this reminder is specifically for fathers as they hold the critical responsibility as head of household, but in my situation as a single mother, I took on this responsibility by default. But really, no mother (single or married) is exempt. Just as the Bible instructs children to obey us (Ephesians 6:1-2), we as parent must not abuse our parental authority. We must strive to treat them with the same dignity, respect, patience, and love that we want from them. Speak in mercy and grace. Forgive quickly. Be open. Be honest. Be vulnerable. Share your experiences with your children. Let your child know your past, who you *are*, not who you want them to see. And heal, woman of God, so that you no longer parent from your traumas and from your wounds. *Amen.*

> "Each time he said, 'My grace is all you need.
> My power works best in weakness.' So now I
> am glad to boast about my weaknesses, so that
> the power of Christ can work through me."
>
> (2 Corinthians 12:9 NLT)

I Heard a Word

What is parenting? What does it mean to raise a child? Why are there so many manuscripts and courses on how to be a better mom, dad, step-parent, adoptive parent? When I tried to read them, I'd often feel worse than before—why didn't I incorporate certain steps earlier or think of those methods beforehand to solve a problem? And, other times, to be perfectly honest, some of the stuff just did not relate culturally or did not speak to my situations at all.

I knew the Bible said to train up a child in the way he should go (Proverbs 22:6), and that *way* is Jesus (John 14:6). Lord knows I tried my best. I made sure we did Bible readings and prayed at home, we went to church together, served the community together, participated in biblical youth programs, camps, everything. These were the very things I remember doing as a child and were beneficial, so naturally, I wanted the same for my children. All of us are a byproduct of who we listen to and whose teaching we are under.

These activities were instilled in me as a child by my parents, and I wanted the same for my children. And it was good. I am sure *good seed* was planted into *good soil* in my children's hearts. What I did not realize at the time, however, was that sometimes I would toss seeds of my own unaddressed pains, doubts, fears, disappointments, sadness, and "stuff" too.

This reminds me of the parable in the Bible in Matthew 13:24-30 where the enemy sowed tares among the wheat. The difference for me was I did not recognize it. I did not realize that the pain was constantly bleeding out into my parenting. I was unknowingly acting like the *foolish* virgins of Matthew 25, like I had enough oil, unprepared until it was perhaps too late.

Wow, ignorance is not really bliss. That's a saying from the pit of hell. So, should I have surprised when my own child called me a hypocrite? Should I have been surprised when my child told me how horrible of a parent I was? Trust me, it was the worse feeling in the world! It made me so enraged!

"How dare they be so ungrateful!"

It made me feel defeated and question myself.

"Where did I go wrong?"

It made me feel sad and disheartened. I wondered,

"Well, maybe I really am the worst parent in the world."

And I got stuck there for a while due to this mindset, these thoughts, and accepting the prophecy spoken to me.

"Why is this happening to me?"

I did everything I could to prevent my children from having the same thoughts and feelings I had toward my parents. At least I had the decency to write down how I felt in a letter addressed to them. These kids nowadays will tell you straight to your face! I could have easily taken offense, shouted, screamed, clapped back, and ran down a list of receipts of all the hypocritical behaviors I noticed in them as well. After all, that is what my parents did to me, so I was ready for it! But, for some reason, I didn't. I stopped myself. I listened. And you know what I heard? I heard *pain*. The same pain I felt had transferred into my children, and now they were crying out:

"Where is the safe place to bleed?"

The answer: it was supposed to have been me. And I was not. And that really woke me up to how important my role was as a mother. How important it is for us to heal for our children's sake so that our children will not have to cry and seek for healing from having us as parents. It was time for me to get to work! And it might be the same for you.

Women of God, heal so that you can hear what is being said without the filter of your wounds. It may not be your fault what happened in your past, but it is your responsibility to get your healing, especially as a parent. Parenting from a wound is *dangerous*. It is *deadly*. This is why the enemy tries to inflict us often—so that we repeat the same cycles of pain from one generation to the next.

No! It stops right here! It stops with you. You are called to be the *repairer of the breach*! This is parenting. You are called to be the *nurse on duty*: to recognize and assess these wounds and to clean these wounds to ensure they heal properly. This is how you raise a child: Stay loyal to your healing.

This job is not for the weak. It gets messy. Our demons live in our wounds. Time to cast them out in Jesus' name. Time to clean them out. It's time to heal, women of God.

As I mentioned before, demons do not respond to prim, proper, and cute, so you better know how to *war*! When you take something by force, you really take it by faith! Your child, your children, will live and not die! Healing affects speaking. *Speak life*! Are you speaking from the *wound* or the *Word?* Immerse yourself in the principles and applications of the World of God! Heal, woman of God! Your faith has made you whole. And it will make your family whole.

> "... *'Daughter, your faith has made you well. Go in peace. Your suffering is over.'"*
>
> (Mark 5:34 NLT)

Loving Even Judas

It amazes me to this day how Jesus was able from the very beginning to look Judas in the eye and welcome him as a disciple, love on him, teach him, make him an apostle, encourage him, call him a brother—despite knowing Judas would betray Him. That takes a special kind of love. To create a whole human race in His image, give us dominion and power over everything in this world that He created, love us, provide for us, protect us, call us His children—despite the fact that we would turn our backs on Him, deny Him, spit in His face, kick Him, beat Him, mock and ridicule Him, and hang Him on a tree. What kind of Father puts up with this?

There is only so much that we as parents can handle from our own children until we break down, retaliate, throw around our authority—lose it. When your child tells you they just want to live their own "truth" and not care about others. When your child tells you that they are gay or feel they were born in the wrong body. When your child tells you that they are using drugs or abusing alcohol. When your child tells you they binge and vomit, but never feel "skinny" enough. When your child tells you they no longer like church, and they don't believe in all that "Jesus stuff" anymore ("it's not for them"). When your child tells you they are pregnant or got somebody pregnant. When they tell you they are moving out, emancipating themselves. It is so *overwhelming*! But not for Jesus. He took on all this and so much more. He took it all because that's how much He loved. He asked God to forgive us because that's how much he loved. He defeated death, hell, and the grave because that's how much He loved.

To this day, He is preparing a place for us in eternity because that's how much He loves. Are you willing to love your children as Christ

loves us?

Are you willing to sacrifice, risk it all for your children to have a better life?

Despite what they say?

Despite what they do?

Are you able to love them unconditionally?

Pray for them even when they hurt you?

Reach out to them when they spitefully use you?

Tell you that you are a horrible parent?

Tell you how much they hate you?

Tell you that you don't know what you are talking about? And that your ways are *archaic*?

Or, maybe, quit talking to you altogether?

Do you have the love of our heavenly Father for all of that?

Lord, I ask and pray that you help us to love as You love. See our children as You see our children. Hear their cries how You hear their cries. Speak as You speak to the root of their issues, the origin of their heart matters.

Help me to love my children unconditionally. Sometimes they make it so hard, and I want to give up. Sometimes I do not understand why they do the things they do or say the things they say. But I give them to You.

Lord, I can't do it on my own. Help me to love them. Lord, You said in Your Word, "though I speak with the tongues of men and angels, but have not love, I have become sounding brass or a clanging symbol" *(1 Corinthians 13:1 NKJV). Lord, I do not want to be a noisy instrument when I come into Your presence or in the presence of my children. I want them to see Your love through me. I want them to hear Your love for them through me. First Corinthians 13:8 says love never fails.*

I cannot fail my children when I truly love. Because love comes from You. You created it. You lived it. You died for it. You rose for it. And You have given it to us to pass down to the next generation. Lord, I come to You like a child myself, with child-like faith. Help me to love my children. May my children love their children. May we see a generation that knows what true love is. What perfect love is. And desire it for themselves and others.

Lord, thank You for your grace, mercy, and love. We do not deserve it, but You give it to us every day, each morning when we wake up—it's been renewed (Lamentations 3:22-23). Help us to parent upon Your principles, guidelines, and precepts. Guide us, Holy Spirit. We love You, Lord. Amen.

> "And now abide faith, hope, love, these
> three; but the greatest of these is love."
>
> (1 Corinthians 13:13 NKJV)

Barabbas vs. Jesus

"For he knew that they handed Him over because of envy."

(Matthew 27:18 NKJV)

We, as women, must be careful of what we pass down to the next generation. The Bible says in Psalm 127:3, that children are a heritage, an inheritance, from the Lord. An inheritance is something that is passed on to another generation. So, if our children in the womb and outside are that valuable, why are we aborting them inside the womb? Why are we not protecting them in homes, locker rooms, bathrooms, their places of education, nor their places of worship? Why would we want to pass on dead children to the next generation? Why would we want to pass on broken children to the next generation? Why would we want to pass on traumatized, molested, mutilated, and confused boys and girls to the next generation? Are we that selfish, that blinded that we cannot see past our current circumstances that we are willing to sacrifice our own children for temporary financial gain? For a degree? For a career? For a man? For a dream? Is it really worth having nothing but ashes to offer the next generation?

In Matthew 27, the crowd in the Bible were willing to crucify Jesus because of their envy of Jesus (v. 18)—so much so that they willingly placed His death and His blood on their hands, and on the hands of their children (v. 25). A whole generation sacrificed because of a selfish "gain"! A whole generation cursed because of temporary insanity. It felt "right" at the moment. It felt "good" at the moment. There was temporary "relief" for the moment. But on the receiving end, someone else suffered. Someone else was sacrificed. Someone else had to *die*.

On the cross, it was Jesus' life. On that abortion table, it was your child's life. On that altar of decision to put your career first, it was your child's future. On that altar to marry someone of the same sex, it was your child's identity. On that altar to chase fame and fortune, it was your child's vision. On that altar to commit adultery, it was your child's stability. On that altar to harm that child physically, mentally, or sexually, it was your child's confidence and self-esteem. On that altar to believe that "man" over your own flesh and blood, it was your child's trust. On that altar to push porn, gender confusion, perversion, and mutilation, it was your child's innocence.

Is this the inheritance you truly want to pass down to the next generation? An inheritance of broken, hurt, confused, and dead, dry bones?

I had a dream one night. I was driving down a familiar road, but it was unusually dark. I had to use my high beams, and when I had turned them on, I saw something white flashing and moving on the right side of the woods. It startled me! I turned the high beams off and back on.

This time, I saw they were little skeletons moving toward the road, climbing over rocks and hills. They were on both sides of the road. I turned the high beams off and on again just to make sure I wasn't seeing things. Once again, they appeared. Needless to say, I picked up speed in my car and drove outta there!

I promise I did not eat anything strange the night before, and I don't do scary movies! I do know that this dream broke my heart because these were the skeletons of little children who were neglected, forgotten, abused, mutilated, and broken. Looking for that glimmer of hope that came from my headlights. They craved for the attention, affection, and nurture that only a mother can give, and once they thought there was a chance of grabbing on to that, it sped away, once again leaving them in the dark. Alone. Helpless. Cold.

What is wrong with us? We as women have everything we need to nurture and care for our children, but when it is time for responsibility, we run away from it! Why is that? Luke 16:15 says, *". . . 'You are those who justify yourselves before men, but God knows your hearts. For what is highly esteemed among men is an abomination in the sight of God"* (NKJV). We began to act, think, look, and become more like the world. That's what happened. We accepted the lie that we need to think and act more like a man to make it in a man's world, denying our own unique strength and capability as women!

We began to crave attention for ourselves, developed the *"forget those kids"* mentality. *"It's time to do me!"* We began to *envy* the time, sacrifice, commitment, attention, and hard work that it takes to raise children, and want it for ourselves. So, we called out for "Barabbas" instead of "Jesus," and we sacrificed and shed blood of the innocent for the pride of life, the lust of the eye, and the lust of the flesh. We gave up our inheritance for a bowl of soup—satisfying in the moment, but leaving us hungry for more and regretful the next day (Genesis 25:29-34). Still leaving you to continue the blood sacrifice. A never-ending and *deadly* cycle.

Women of God, we must *repent*! Tear down these altars! Our God is a jealous God, and we should have no other gods before Him (Exodus 34:12-14). We have brought judgment on ourselves and our children. We have made *unholy* covenants on *unholy* altars with the god of this world that must be renounced, torn down, and broken. We must get back into *holy* covenant with our Lord and Savior Jesus Christ. It is not too late for the salvation God has for you. It is not too late for the salvation of your children. And your next generation can be healed, set free, and delivered. They can live again!

How? By women taking their rightful place back in their homes and becoming the nurturers, life-givers, prayer warriors, and caretakers of their families and the next generation. By women submitting to the will of our heavenly Father. By women adorning themselves with humility, modesty, and self-control. By women being respectable members of society and our communities who keep the peace.

We fight for the safety and protection of our children. We honor and respect our husbands and our fathers. We do not let just any man plant their seed in us, but we *wait* and *accept* wisely the man that God has in store for us. We study the Word of God and hide it in our hearts so that we do not sin against God (Psalm 119:11). We rebuke the devil and remember that God honors covenant. We plead the blood of Jesus over our children. We declare Isaiah 7:7 that whatever the enemy has been lying to us about—it shall not stand, and it shall not come to pass! We cry out to God to replace what is broken. We ask God to make us visionary and reveal to us what is wrong and replace it. Make it like it never happened! We fast and pray! We *stay on the matter*! We stay in covenant with the one true God: Jesus Christ, Yeshua Hamashiach! We stay covered by God! And we stay on the post as the *repairer of the breach* and *watchers* of our homes, our children, and our inheritance. *Amen.*

> " . . . *You shall raise up the foundations of many generations; And you shall be called the Repairer of the Breach, . . .* "

(Isaiah 58:12 NKJV)

Healing Waters

THE VISION

- ❖ Pathway leading to dark, bare tree. And, an unformed substance hovering over it, and holding it in its hands, like claws, like a crystal ball.

FOUNDATION OF THE VISION

- ❖ No fruit (bare tree)

    Just enough light to see the truth
    Only one way
- ❖ Matthew 13:22, "Now he who received seed [the Word] among the thorns is he who hears the word, and the cares of this world and the deceitfulness of riches choke the word, and he becomes <u>unfruitful</u>" (NKJV, emphasis added).

- 2 Corinthians 4:4, "whose minds the god of this age has blinded, who do not believe, lest the light of the gospel of the glory of Christ, who is the image of God, should shine on them" (NKJV).

THE FLOW

I never realized how often the Bible writes about trees and water in the Bible until recently. One night, God brought me to a particular chapter: Ezekiel 47. Go ahead and take some time to read it before going on. It will help everything make sense. Afterward, God directed me to read Psalm 1:3. Go ahead and read that verse too.

Now, I do not know what God had revealed to you, but I will share my revelation based on the vision of the bare tree I had mentioned at the beginning of this chapter. Once again, this bare tree represents us: out of the will of God, weak, without the Word. But once we get the Word of God represented by light into us, the light begins to expose those hindrances and delays for us. Once exposed, we are able to uproot and cast away anything in our soul (mind, will, intellect, and emotion) that does not glorify God. How do we do this? Very simple:

- Pray for the Circumcision of Our Hearts:
  - Ask God to uproot any unholy, ungodly memory out of our hearts and make it like it never happened. Ask God to uproot bitterness, hatred, unforgiveness, wickedness, perversion, lying, adultery, fornication, murder, laziness, procrastination, forgetfulness, worry, doubt, anxiety, fear, theft, suicidal ideation, gossip, abortion, witchcraft, lesbianism, bestiality, pornography, yoga, sororities, backsliding . . . etc.
- Speak the Word of God:
  - Matthew 3:10 (NKJV), "... *the ax is laid to the root of the trees.*" Ask the Holy Spirit to take the ax to those roots.
- Boldly:
  - *It's all in the frequency of your voice)* curse those roots and command them to be plucked up:

- They must obey you because you have the same power of Jesus inside of you.
- Matthew 21:21 (NKJV) says, "... *'if you have faith, and do not doubt, you will not only do what was done to the fig tree, but also if you say to this mountain 'Be removed and be cast into the sea,' it will be done."*

Now we know once something has been uprooted, it dies. And this is where we ask God to loose restoration upon us with the blood of Jesus so that our foundation in Christ may be cleansed, holy, and righteous. That we may be like the tree in Psalm 1:3, planted by rivers of water.

- ❖ Decree and declare that the year of drought will no longer apply to you.
- ❖ Remind God of His Word in Proverbs 12:3, that the roots of the righteous shall not be moved. This is holy ground.
- ❖ Pray, "I am planted by the rivers of healing water that flows from the sanctuary of heaven" (from Ezekiel 47). Pray to be covered and washed by the Word.
- ❖ Pray and declare, "Not only am I healed, but those around me, my children, my family, my loved ones will be healed and live."
  - Ezekiel 47:9 (NKJV), "... *every living thing that moves ... wherever the rivers go, will live."*
- ❖ Thank God for His blessings that come from being planted along the banks of the river:
  - I will grow as all kinds of trees used for food.
  - My leaves will not wither but shall be used for medicine (health and healing properties for my mind, soul, and body).
  - My fruit will not fail; I will bear the fruit of the Holy Spirit.
  - I will bear fruit every month:
    - ✦ I will prosper in every season and not be delayed.
    - ✦ I will function as designed.

- My womb will be open and bear children as designed.
- I will be *fruitful* and multiply as God commanded.

Isn't it a beautiful thing to know the Lord and be in His will? Psalm 63:1-2 beautifully depicts why it is so important to be in the *sanctuary*, the *refuge*, the *holy place*, the *Lord Himself*. Because it is in Him where we are safe, we are whole, we are healed, and we are blessed. From the sanctuary is a dependable water supply essential for life and for defense. From the sanctuary is flowing streams that are *parables* of the flowing life of God. Our Father God cares about the environment (of your life) and promises to restore and heal it. If we follow Jesus, we will live, our children will live, and our future generations will live. Let's parent from healing, restoration, and righteousness. *Amen.*

> *"How beautiful on the mountains are the feet of the messenger who brings good news, the good news of peace and salvation, the news that the God of Israel reigns!"*
>
> (Isaiah 52:7 NLT)

Journal Journey Entries

ENTRY

How I feel as a mother right now: no respect . . . no trust . . . no emotions . . . abandonment . . . not loved.

Tears streaming down my face, my heart broken into pieces, hurting. I have not heard from God. He seems distant. I cry into my pillow, "Jesus, please help me! Where are You? I can't hear You! I don't know what to do. I feel like a failure. I'm afraid. My children hate me, and I don't know why. What did I do wrong? What did I do to hurt them so bad? I can't talk with them. They won't let me in. I need help!"

Psalm 61:1-2 (NKJV):

> "Hear my cry, O God; Attend to my prayer.
> From the end of the earth, I will cry to
> You, When my heart is overwhelmed; Lead
> me to the rock that is higher than I."

It's hard to give respect when you do not feel respected. It is hard to trust when it is broken inside. It is hard to show emotions when raised to show none. It's hard to love when not shown what it looks like. It's hard to be there for someone when all you've known was abandonment.

Children are reflections of us—our good, our bad, our ugly. They mirror all of our imperfections, inner wounds, traumas, joys, pains, and self-concept. What they put out is what they see in you. *Heal.*

ENTRY

Stop running from fights! Motherhood includes warring in the spirit for our children. Do not leave the next generation after you to deal with your unfinished combat! Learn how to push your plate, fast, pray, and *war*!

ENTRY

It's so hard to help someone through something that you have not yet healed from yourself. To see and watch your child struggle with the very same thing you do and have no answers is very painful. It's scary! You begin to doubt your capability as a parent. *Why do I even want to do this? Why did I ever want to do this?* No one tells you about this when you become a parent. You get all caught up in the "fluff" of parenting, with all the baby showers and outfits and picking a name, but no one asks if you are mentally ready to have a child. Have you healed from your past wounds? Are you holding resentment against your mom or dad or any other relative? These things don't magically go away. They can easily roll right into your own parenting.

We try so hard to do the opposite of however our parents raised us. Yet those toxic habits just fly out and transcend into our movements, behaviors, and handling of certain situations with our kids.

Lord, help me to hear the natural and the spiritual cries of my children. Help me to discern what it is that they need from me when they speak. Help me to hear them in their silence.

Lord, help me to be a place of safety for them and not harm. Lord, as their first teacher in life, please help me to accept and realize that I was operating out of a place of ignorance. And now that You have shown me the way, truth, and life, I can help bring healing to their land as well.

Lord, break this generational momentum that these wounds have caused. May it never pick back up again. My children shall live and not die! They have been purchased with the blood of Christ, and they are God's children.

Thank You, God, for their healing, their restoration, their joy, and their happiness in you. May they enter Your Kingdom and experience the eternity you prepared for them since birth. You love them more than I ever could. Bless them and keep them. In Jesus' name. Amen.

ENTRY

Parenting Strategy: Part I

- ❖ The enemy never wants us to reach maturity, so he uses childhood trauma. Healing is so important. Hell gets terrified when we evolve and heal. Ask God to give you discernment during your healing process. Counterfeits always seek to disrupt your evolution and your healing process. Stay vigilant! Remaining carnal is so hazardous. Build spiritual fortitude in the Word of God. Deal with the shame, failure, evil thoughts, and lies that hell has implanted. No more running. Stand your ground! Armor up! (Ephesians 6:12-19).

- ❖ The enemy wants your wounds to have generational momentum. Many of us are fighting the unfinished combat of our parents, grandparents, great-grandparents and elsewhere in our family trees. It must end here! Women of God, we need to know who we are in Christ Jesus and whose we are. Our confidence is tied to authenticity, anointing, and power! Our heavenly Father knows and receives the sound of our cry and responds! The enemy wants you to go mute and die! Our heavenly Father wants to redeem the inner child and make us whole. Not just "happy." Happiness is not a fruit of the the Holy Spirit. Let's be more like a child to experience the miraculous to enter the joy of the Lord. Let's forgive our first teachers, our parents, our guardians who taught us wrong, who taught us lessons that were not Kingdom. The cycle ends with us!

- ❖ Untreated trauma and pain will blur our discernment. We begin to blame the person and not the pattern. Untreated trauma and pain rewires us to self-preserve and close up. No! Reach out and get help! Talk about it! When we keep it inside, we become miserable. "When I kept silent, my bones grew old Through my groaning all the day long" (Psalm 32:3 NKJV). Forgive yourself. Forgive others. Go to counseling. What has not been rehabilitated will get recycled. Unlearn that abuse. Unlearn those survival tactics that become your personality. You will no longer be your wound. I am healed. I am healing. I am whole in Jesus' name. I will live and not die! Amen.

- ❖ Have patience in the healing process. We must trust God's pace. Allow God to redeem your inner child.

- ❖ When children go silent, look for them and help them. This is not normal behavior. Warfare is raging. Sound the alarms, women of God!

- ❖ Surround yourself with songs of deliverance! Whatever song or passage God places in your heart and mind at that moment, sing it out loud! It doesn't matter if you have the vocals or not. The Lord said to make a joyful noise! Don't let that excuse be a distraction in your ear. Rebuke it! That song at that moment can set you free! Rescue you from actual or delayed evil! Save you! Save your children! Work out that situation! Release that generational curse! Produce the promise! And heal the wounds! Get the Word of God in you so that those songs can pour out like balm to your dry, thirsty soul, sealant to your open wounds, and peace over your mind, body, will, and emotions. Songs of deliverance are real instruments of divine grace.

    - ○ *"You are my hiding place; You shall preserve me from trouble; You shall surround me with songs of deliverance. Selah."* (Psalm 32:7 NKJV)

- *"The Lord will command His loving-kindness in the daytime, And in the night His song shall be with me—A prayer to the God of my life."* (Psalm 42:8 NKJV)

ENTRY

Parenting Strategy: Part II

- ❖ Live right: It protects your kids. They live blessed lives when we live right.
  - Follow God's rules and laws in the Word of God. Hide it in your heart so that you don't sin (Psalm 119:11).
  - The seed of the righteous shall be delivered (Proverbs 11:21).
  - The generation of the upright will be blessed (Psalm 112:1-3).
- ❖ Remember that we do not live for ourselves.
  - Pray for God to rule on behalf of your children and not just yourself.
  - Pray Scripture. You will get results.
  - God's Word does not return void (Isaiah 55:11).
- ❖ Pray for your child's salvation—not for riches, fame, and superficial things.
  - Give my child eternal life in You, Jesus, so that no one can snatch them out of Your hand (John 10:28).
  - Remove my child's heart of stone and give him or her a heart of flesh, Lord. Put a new spirit in them (Ezekiel 36:26).
  - Let my child hear Your voice when you call and recognize it as the voice of the Good Shepherd (John 10:27).
  - Lord, make my child's heart good soil that will receive the seed and produce grain a hundred-fold (Matthew 13:8).
  - Lord, draw my child to Yourself and raise them up on the last day (John 6:44).

- ○ Lord, write my child's name in the Lamb's Book of Life (Revelation 21:27).
- ❖ Remember that as we mature, we must become fervent in our prayer. As we mature, the attacks on us become greater.
  - ○ Pray against every attack of the enemy.
  - ○ *"The weapons of our warfare are not carnal but mighty in God for pulling down strongholds."* (2 Corinthians 10:4 NKJV)
- ❖ Pray that our children be good husbands and wives.
  - ○ Have success in the creation roles that God deemed in His creation (Genesis 2:18-24).
  - ○ What *God* joins together, let no one separate (Mark 10:9).
  - ○ Owe no one anything, except to love each other, for the one who loves another fulfilled the Law (Romans 13:8).
- ❖ Even in dysfunctional upbringing, God can work on your behalf if you are steadfast and willing to give yourself up for them.
  - ○ *"Train up a child in the way he should go, And when he is old he will not depart from it."* (Proverbs 22:6 NKJV)
- ❖ Pray for the other parent and believe God for them, doing right by the children.
  - ○ Pray against the spirit of anger, revenge, malice, and seditious behaviors that damage the children inside and outside the womb.
  - ○ Pray for the heart of the fathers to their children (Luke 1:17).
- ❖ Pray for God's benefits for our children:
  - ○ **Top Education:** *"All your children shall be taught by the Lord, And great shall be the peace of your children"* (Isaiah 54:13 NKJV).
  - ○ **Endurance:** *". . . And His truth endures to all generations"* (Psalm 100:5 NKJV).
- ❖ **Long Life:** *". . . 'Honor your father and mother' is the first commandment that has a <u>promise</u> attached to it, namely, 'so that*

you will live well and have a long life'" (Ephesians 6:2-3 MSG, emphasis added).

❖ **Inheritance & Generational Wealth:** *" . . . And your descendants will inherit the nations, And make the desolate cities inhabited"* (Isaiah 54:3 NKJV).

❖ **Ministry:** *"And in the last days it shall be, God declares, that I will pour out my Spirit on all flesh, and your sons and your daughters shall prophesy, and your young men shall see visions, and your old men shall dream dreams"* (Acts 2:17 ESV).

❖ War against the enemy for your children!
  ○ Isaiah 54:15 (NKJV), *"Indeed they shall surely assemble but not because of Me. Whoever assembles against you shall fall for your sake."*
  ○ Isaiah 54:17, *"No weapon formed against you shall prosper, And every tongue which rises against you in judgment You shall condemn . . . "*
  ○ Colossians 2:15, *"Having disarmed principalities and powers, He made a public spectacle of them, triumphing over them in it."*
  ○ Psalm 23:6, *"Surely goodness and mercy shall follow me* [and my children] *all the days of my life* [their lives] *and I* [we] *will dwell in the house of the Lord Forever"*

  Amen.

ENTRY

Have you ever imagined what it would ever be like to be the earthly mother of Jesus? Sometimes I do wonder what it would be like to never have to discipline my children, correct them, or punish them. Sounds amazing, right? Yet, she still had to teach Him how to grow up in a sense, such as teaching Him how to wash His face, brush His teeth, use his food utensils, how to walk . . . etc. I bet it was so surreal.

I wonder if she ever got caught up in the moment of joy when He hit milestones like His first tooth or birthday, and then it would hit her out the blue that this was the Son of God that she was raising! In a sense, she really didn't have to "teach" Him *anything* because He was all-knowing, but she still had to teach Him *everything*!

I wonder if she ever slipped up and compared her other children to Jesus and asked them, "Why can't you be like your big brother, Jesus? He never did or said that!" Like, how did she do it? I could only imagine how she felt when she and Joseph accidentally left Jesus behind in Jerusalem at twelve years old, thinking He was with other family members. (I can relate to the sheer panic when I lost my son at the state fair, thinking he was with another family member). And not only did they find this youngin' sitting and inquiring with the teachers and professors of the First Temple of the Latter-Day Saints, but He had the nerve to tell them, "Why were you looking for me? I am out here doing my Father's business. Huh? Like what?

See, this is why neither you nor I were chosen to be Mary. We probably would have snatched little Jesus up, right then and there, and caused a whole scene! But just reading her responses and observing her temperance in Scripture really amazes me. I am sure it was hard for her to let Him grow up and fulfill His calling with images in her mind of Him being a small, helpless baby who needed her. But because she knew her own assignment and purpose, she was able to raise the most perfect *man* that the world has ever come to know.

Because Jesus' parents submitted to the will of God, Jesus also submitted to His earthly parents. This is why it is so important for us as mothers to remember who we are in Christ Jesus and live righteously—so that we can raise our children to know whose they are and become strong in the Spirit, filled with wisdom and the grace of God upon them (Luke 2:40).

Even after little Jesus reminded His parents of why He was there on earth, the Bible says in Luke 2:51 that Jesus was subject to them, became dependent upon them, and still submitted under their authority. And it was because of Mary's obedience, her temperance, her willingness, her faith, her love, and her trust in the Word that was given to her about who Jesus was. Jesus increased in wisdom and stature because of Mary and in favor with God and man (Luke 2:52). This can be the outcome of our children as well.

Let's be more like the Mary, who became more like Jesus when she gave life: Jesus came to give life and give it more abundantly (John 10:10). Let's be more like the Mary, who said to the workers at the wedding feast: " . . . 'Whatever He says to you, do it'" (John 2:5 NKJV). That's confidence and faith in the Savior. Let's be more like the Mary, who was positioned in submission, holiness, righteousness, and favor with God so that we can become impregnated with the Word of God (Luke 1:30). Let's be the mother who is called "blessed" when others come in contact with our children (Luke 11:27). Let's be mothers who are in constant prayer for our families (Acts 1:14). And let's be mothers who are slow to speak and quick to listen (Luke 2:19). *Amen.*

ENTRY

I was listening to a profound sermon one day that grabbed my attention. The pastor said each and every one of us has been ordained before conception. The medical community tells us that life begins at conception, but the Word of God tells us that life starts at ordination.

> *"Thus says the Lord who made you*
> *And formed you from the womb, who will help you: . . .*
> *I will pour My Spirit on your descendants,*
> *And My blessing on your offspring;*
> *They will spring up among the grass*
> *Like willows by the watercourses.'"*
>
> (Isaiah 44:2-4 NKJV)

The word "spring" means to come from birth or descent. God was blessing our children and giving them orders *before* they came from birth or were conceived. Before they were even a thought in our minds, He was giving them marching orders to fulfill on this earth. So, who are we to get in the way? How dare we abort that mission! How dare we terminate that plan! How dare we make ourselves "god" and issue out an alternative, satanic order, a pharaoh or Haman's decree?! These children have orders to grow and be prosperous. These children have orders to have the Spirit of God manifest through them: the spirit of love, joy, peace, patience, kindness, goodness, faithfulness, gentleness, and self-control. All the things this world needs. These children bring innocence in the purest form from the heavenly Father. Why do you think the devil is coming so fiercely after our children? Could you imagine how much better our world would be today if those millions of aborted babies were alive?

Women of God, our children are our blessing. Regardless of the circumstances within which they were given to us, they are our blessing to the world. Protect them!

First Timothy 2:15 (NKJV) says, "... *she will be saved in childbearing if they continue in faith, love, and holiness, with self-control.*"

Having children is a blessing, not a curse. Do not fall for that evil, wicked lie of the enemy. Through our obedience to accept this responsibility, through our faith that God will provide, through our love for that child and others, through our righteousness, our children will save us, save the next generation, and preserve life. They have orders from God to do so. Let go of that control and let God's perfect will take place. Let salvation pour like living water through this dry and thirsty land. The souls of our children are crying for this living water. Let's allow this healing to flow instead of the cry of innocent bloodshed. Let's allow our dry, thirsty souls to drink from the cup of life. *Amen.*

"For I will pour water on him who is thirsty,
And floods on the dry ground;"

(Isaiah 44:4 NKJV)

ENTRY

I remember watching a nature movie with my daughter one evening that showed the difficulties and journeys of baby animals in the wild. Some of the stories were inspiring, some courageous, and others sad. But there was one that was so random and caught us both off guard. The life of the baby cuckoo bird.

We watched in horror how the mother bird not only dropped off her single egg into the other birds' nest full of eggs and flew away never to return, but when the baby bird hatched before the other eggs in the nest, that baby bird pushed the other eggs out the nest! To make the story even worse and traumatic, the mother bird whose nest was infiltrated did not even seem to notice how much different and much bigger this baby bird was. It was so demanding of food, but the mother bird did all she could to keep up with its demands. There were days that it would pour down rain, and this mother bird would spread herself thin to try to cover this big bird more than half her size! My daughter and I could not believe it! I had never heard of such a thing before. Like, wow!

Months later, God brought this memory back to me and I looked up this type of bird, and there were others like this one, all parasitic in nature. This was their life strategy used to pass on their genes to the next generation. What parasitic behavior have we passed on into our children? Matthew 6:12 (NKJV) says, *"And forgive us our debts, As we forgive our debtors."* We have to know when we are in the wrong. We have to recognize when we are the offenders. We have to pay attention to our words, actions, and behaviors. When it comes to our children, what is in us gets passed down to them:

- ❖ Do we harbor unforgiveness?
    - ○ Matthew 5:7 (NKJV), *"Blessed are the merciful, For they shall obtain mercy."*
    - ○ Obtain mercy from the Lord, and pray it over your children.
- ❖ Are you proud? Boastful?
    - ○ Micah 6:8, *"He has shown you, O man, what is good; And what does the Lord require of you But to do justly, To love mercy, And to walk humbly with your God?"*
    - ○ Walk humbly and exemplify it before your children.
- ❖ Are you envious or jealous?
    - ○ 1 Peter 2:1-2, *"Therefore, laying aside all malice, all deceit, hypocrisy, envy and all evil speaking, as newborn babies desire the pure milk of the word, that you may grow thereby."*
    - ○ Lay it aside so that you may be satisfied in God, and your children can grow up into the salvation of the Lord.
- ❖ Are you a liar or manipulator?
    - ○ Proverbs 30:5, *"Every word of God is pure; He is a shield to those who put their trust in Him."*

- Put into practice speaking the Word of God and speak it over your children daily.

❖ Have you committed murder and/or had an abortion?
- Proverbs 18:21, *"Death and life are in the power of the tongue, And those who love it will eat its fruit."*
- Use your mouth to speak death to the spirit of abortion and murder. Close that door. No longer may it use your wounds as an open door to hurt you or your children. Plead the blood of Jesus. Place the cross between all the past, present, and future generations. Every curse and assignment must stop at the cross. Speak life! And eat its fruit.

❖ Are you a gossiper or instigator?
- Proverbs 11:13 (ESV), *"Whoever goes about slandering reveals secrets, but he who is trustworthy in spirit keeps a thing covered."*
- Be a woman of God who is trustworthy, prays, and fasts in the Spirit, and keeps herself, her home, and her family covered. *Amen.*

ENTRY

There are times in our lives where we fail;
There are times in our life where we are victorious;
There are times in our lives where we do not understand;
There are times in our lives where we have direction;
There are times in our lives where we hear God;
There are times where He is silent.

But even in the silence, He speaks;
The silence tells us He is listening;
The silence tells us He is there;
The silence reminds us,
that we must fully surrender

our will to His to continue on;
When He is silent,
we must be still.

Quiet our thoughts,
Quiet our fears,
Quiet ourselves,
And listen.

It is in the silence that
His mysteries are revealed to us.
It is in the silence that our eyes are opened
To the truth of our situations,
To the bigger picture of our circumstances.
It is in the silence that our pride is broken;
Humbleness covers us.

It is the time that healing comes.
Be grateful for the silence;
welcome the silence.
It is the time when God speaks the loudest
without saying a word.

Pray
Be still
And know that His is God
Amen.

~Psalm 46:10~

ENTRY

A lesson in motherhood: the self-centered woman can never find fulfillment of joy. The Christ-like life is the continuing process of spiritual growth through self-denial. We must be okay that it is no longer about us when it comes to becoming a mother. We must be okay with the biblical principle that it is more blessed to give than to receive (Acts 21:35). When living a life of selflessness, we as mothers can find the true fulfillment and joy in Jesus, and our children will rise up and call us blessed (Proverbs 31:28).

ENTRY

Return and Be Healed

~Isaiah 6:10~

Sometimes our children drift away,
Sometimes they stay.
Sometimes we wonder if they will ever return;
Sometimes they never recover from the hurt.
Sometimes they ask us for direction;
Sometimes they won't.
Sometimes they look at us straight like we are crazy.
Sometimes they admire from afar.
Sometimes our children forget,
Sometimes they remember.
Sometimes they will call,
Sometimes not.
Sometimes our children hug us,
Sometimes they run from our embrace.
Sometimes our children are helpful,
Sometimes they are not.
Sometimes our children will nap,
Sometimes they refuse.
Sometimes they follow the rules;
Sometimes they rebel.
Sometimes our children love church;
Sometimes they try to forget God.
Sometimes they remember your birthday,
Sometimes sing you a song.
Sometimes they will put on a talent show,
Sometimes fall out in a tantrum.
Sometimes our children slam the door;
Sometimes they yell in frustration.

Sometimes they are confused.
Sometimes they just don't know.
Sometimes you and I are these children.
We need the guidance, love, and care from our heavenly Father.
We need to be like a child,
Open, vulnerable, trusting,
Dependent on an
Ever- lasting
Always- present
All- knowing
Savior and Friend.
We need to *return and be healed*,
We need to be humble.
Come back home, My daughter, My son,
Jesus has been waiting.
Amen.

> "... Lest they see with their eyes,
> And hear with their ears,
> And understand with their heart,
> And return and be healed."
>
> (Isaiah 6:10 NKJV)

ENTRY

I remember having a FaceTime conversation with my sister about my niece. In the middle of that conversation, my niece did something she was not supposed to, and my sister had to correct her with a stern voice. I watched how my niece instantly burst into tears and then ran to her mother for a hug. My sister started laughing and commented how her daughter does the opposite of what most kids do when they get in trouble. Most kids run away or hide from the person who catches them doing wrong! I thought it was interesting, realizing that *all* of us need to be more like my little niece. When she gets scolded or in trouble, she cries and runs toward the one correcting her, not away. When we get corrected or in trouble, we need to run to our Daddy, Jesus, and embrace that correction in trust and surrender.

Matthew 18:3-4 (ESV) says, "*. . . 'unless you turn and become like children, you will never enter the kingdom of heaven. Whoever humbles himself like a child is the greatest in the kingdom of heaven.'"* This is a great reminder that we need to become more like a child. Get rid of the fear, the pride, the anger, the frustration, the resentment, the hatred, the grudges, etc. Drop it and run to Jesus.

Once we get corrected, we get loved. Once my niece ran to my sister, she was embraced and loved on. Same with God: He corrects us and then loves us. Do not be afraid of correction; embrace it. *"For the Lord disciplines those He loves and punishes each one he accepts as his child"* (Hebrews 12:6 NLT).

It hurts to be corrected, yes! It's painful. My niece expressed that pain with her outburst of tears. It was in that outburst that the release came through; she did not hold on to it, allowing it to fester inside or turn into something dark and ugly as a wound. No! She let it go! It is okay to release, whether that be in tears, a yell, a scream, a full-blown tantrum (I've done them all). Whatever it takes, let that hurt go! Allow that pain to release. And then embrace that one who loved you so much to stop you from going into that direction, that place, that relationship, that situation, that dead-end street, that bad decision, or that misstep which was going to cause you more harm than good.

It is in that embrace that the change comes. I noticed my niece calm down, begin to smile, and then hug her mother back. It was such a heartfelt scene to watch both of them smiling together. It is in that embrace where we begin to feel the love, forgiveness, and mercy of God washing over us. We become just like a child. This is the place where Christ wants us. Humble. When we are humble, we become more Christ-like. We look more like Christ: we take on His attributes, actions, mannerisms—just like a child who mimics their parents. We become God's little Mini-Mes. And this is our key into the Kingdom of heaven.

Let's become more like our children, women of God. Let's release, heal, and embrace the process of correction instead of running from it. Let's humble ourselves and focus on being great in the Kingdom of heaven. *Amen.*

ENTRY

God gave me a verse one day out of nowhere, and I wrote it down, but was not quite sure why:

*"Awake you who sleep, Arise from the
dead, And Christ will give you light."*

(Ephesians 5:14 NKJV)

It wasn't until months later that He gave me the revelation about it. I was doing a random search about sycamore trees after hearing a discussion about them in a message online. They are large trees with aggressive, deep, and wide-spreading roots. These trees are highly adaptable and resilient. They also don't require a lot of light or water to grow in the summer months and dry periods. These gigantic trees were used by the Egyptians to carve out coffins for the mummies. All interesting, right? Well, then God began to show me how many of us have a lot of deep-rooted feelings and emotions, just like this tree, that are toxic and slowly destroying us. Deep roots of depression, anxiety, resentment, anger, hatred, bitterness, unforgiveness, fear, grief, sadness, jealousy, rage, pride, and regret.

These roots are so firmly rooted deep inside our hearts that we speak death to ourselves, our own children, and others around us. Instead of giving life, we are producing caskets. Instead of the favorable conditions of moist soil and sunlight, we prefer darkness and drought. For some reason, we find pleasure in self-inflicted wounds and bleeding out on those around us. We are sick and dying on the inside while trying to appear majestic on the outside.

We sleep, smoke, and drink our lives away, hoping that life will pass us by because that's easier than facing reality. That temporary high and numbing makes it a little easier to deal with. No! Enough! This is not the life God has planned for you. This is a delusion! Wake up!

*"Awake, you who sleep, Arise from the dead.
And Christ will give you the light."*

God is calling you, women of God. He wants to do a good work in you. He loves you. He thinks you are special. And He wants you to live a blessed and abundant life. It is not too late. It is *never* too late. What the enemy has lied to you about shall not stand, and it will not come to pass (Isaiah 7:7). You will live and not die! Your children will live and not die! Your family will live and not die!

It is time to repent and ask the Holy Spirit to take the battle ax and chop this tree down and uproot it. Plant some good seed from the Word of God in your heart. Study it, memorize it, let that grow in you. Let's grow in favorable conditions and produce life.

Ephesians 5:8-9 (NKJV) says, *"For you were once darkness, but now you are the light in the Lord. Walk as children of light (for the fruit of the Spirit is in all goodness, righteousness, and truth)."* The favor of God is upon us, women of God. Let's walk in our anointing, stay close to God, and continue to be rooted in the Word of God. *Amen.*

ENTRY

> *"And go quickly and tell His disciples that He is risen from the dead, and indeed He is going before you into Galilee; there you will see Him . . . "*
>
> (Matthew 28:7 NKJV)

> *"Then the eleven disciples went away into Galilee, to the mountain which Jesus had appointed for them."*
>
> (Matthew 28:16)

Many of us lose our way and try to return to the dead place. Many of us were given instructions from God, but we doubted. Many of us are bringing incenses and fragrances of prayer to try to resurrect a dead situation. We desire to return back to Egypt because "at least we ate good," forgetting about the slavery and chains that sin had us bound in.

We search these dead places, people, and things for an answer, but it is all in vain. That's because that place is not *appointed* for you. Do not return to the dead place- but go to the place that God *appointed* where you may *live*! Ask God to show you where your *Galilee* is so that you will see Him and receive your instruction, your power, your authority, your purpose! Go to Galilee, woman of God! Make haste! See God and live! Amen.

> "... 'Go and tell my brethren to go to Galilee, and there they will see Me.'"
>
> (Matthew 28:10 NKJV)

ENTRY

Let's pray, women of God, to be the first in line of miracles for our bloodline, for the next generation, and the many generations to follow. In the Old Testament, Elijah raised a widow's son from the dead (1 Kings 17). This *never* happened before! This can be our testimony as well! We will be the first to have a Kingdom marriage. We will be the first to raise Kingdom-minded children. We will be the first to build, create, and pass on generational wealth. We will be the first to be healed from those familial diseases and illness. We will be the first to be in our right mind. We will be the first to break the mold. We will be the first in line for our breakthrough! Be healed, have faith, pray intentionally and specifically, and expect great things! *Amen.*

ENTRY

Parenting requires fighting power. This cannot be acquired from a victim perspective. We cannot keep looking back and blaming our parents, our upbringing, and our circumstances.

> *Let that go! Forgive. Repent. Heal!*

Make the choice to do it God's way and follow His rules, His commandments, and His principles in His Word. When you choose and try to do good, evil can and will challenge you every time, so be ready for it (Romans 7:21-23).

> "Do not be overcome by evil, but over-

> *come evil with good."*
>
> (Romans 12:21 NKJV)

Now, how do we do that? We change our perspective. We change our mindset:

1. Romans 12:2 tells us not to be conformed (molded) to how the world does things. Being Christ followers and women of God requires us to have a distinctive character that will never fit in any mold the world tries to offer. You will never fit. Stop fighting to fit in. Have respect for yourself. Be unique in Christ Jesus. Be satisfied with that. Know who you are in Christ Jesus. That is *fighting power* against the enemy!

2. Romans 12:2 also says to be transformed (changed). Transformation requires a healing process. We cannot fight wounded, blinded, broken, and disgusted with a defeated mindset. No! We must plead and release the healing blood of Jesus into our own lives and our parenting situations. The blood of Jesus speaks life and healing. By His stripes we are healed and made whole (Isaiah 53:5). This is our *fighting power* against the enemy.

3. Lastly, Romans 12:2 says transformation comes by renewing our minds. When we heal, our minds are set free, and the renewal process can begin. We have the ability to be restored in our right minds. We become new in mind, body, will, and emotions. We are able to receive fresh insight from the Word of God and become *strong* again! That's *more fighting power* against the enemy!

> *"Finally, my brethren, be strong in the Lord and in the power of His might."*
>
> (Ephesians 6:10 NKJV)
>
> *Amen.*

ENTRY

Sometimes, when it is late in the hour, you are on the brink of your breakthrough, your joy is about to come in the morning, and in comes all the worry, doubt, fear, frustration, confusion, procrastination, anxiety— all the emotions that strategically cause delay and distraction.

At some point, we have got to get tired of this same old play thrown out by the devil and call it out for what it is. At some point, we have got to make it a habit not to entertain these thoughts but *immediately* get on our knees and cry out to God. We need to ask that He remove our property off the enemy radar! At this point, we need to speak the Word according to Isaiah 7:7—that whatever the enemy has been lying to us about will *not* stand and it shall *not* come to pass! Complete and permanent deliverance from this point on!

Feelings shift, but faith is fixed. Fixed on Jesus so much that we stay focused on His Word, His promises, until no other voice matters to us. The voice of all those other emotions won't matter. No one and nothing can deter us:

- ✓ No, fear! You cannot distract me. Fear involves torment, but perfect love casts out fear (1 John 4:18).
- ✓ I declare the God of Intervention will intercede in my life and in my children's lives right now in Jesus' name. I release the blood of Jesus over us and our breakthrough!
- ✓ I call on Jehovah Nissi, the Lord my banner (Exodus 17:15).
- ✓ I speak to each and every mountain in my way to be removed and cast into the sea (Matthew 17:20).

This is the faith we need to receive our breakthrough. Faith without works (for ourselves, our children, and our future generations) is dead faith. Keep pressing through. Keep moving forward. And get your breakthrough healing, daughter of the Most High King.

> *"'Daughter,' he said to her, 'your faith has made you well. Go in peace.'"*
>
> (Luke 8:48 NLT).
>
> Amen.

ENTRY

There is a sad story in 2 Samuel 4 about a child named Mephibosheth who was dropped by the nurse carrying him, and as a result, became crippled. He was five years old. It made me think that even though this happened in physically, this can happen to us spiritually and in our children. We must be careful who we let carry, influence mentally/emotionally, or have access to our children. Not every "nurse" or person entrusted to take care of our children has good intentions, or even if they do, they can become reckless and careless to a point that they cause detrimental and crippling effects on our children's mental, physical, and spiritual well-being.

We must cover our children in prayer daily, no matter their age. We must have conversations with our children constantly, no matter how uncomfortable it may be. We must make ourselves available to them, no matter what the costs. They are our ministry. The devil is after our children, and if he can steal their identity at a very young age, he will do it. If he can send an agent of the enemy to lure your child away while you are busy living your "best life," he will gladly step in. If he can get in the sound-waves and airways of your child's entertainment outlets, he will take over. If he can use your child's best friend, school counselor, church youth group leader, family member, or any other entrusted family friend to plant a single seed of confusion, death, and fear to cripple their sense of worth, innocence, and hope, he will at any costs.

Our children are the closest thing to God, and the enemy knows it. That is why it is so important that we intercede on the behalf of our children every moment we can. We must speak up and speak out for the protection of our children from every evil agenda and attack being made against them. We cannot afford our future generations to be crippled by fear, confusion, anger, hatred, anxiety, and depression. *No!* The enemy will not have our children. They will live and not die! We will plead the blood of Jesus over our children! They will grow strong in the Lord. They will not fall prey to the evil schemes of the enemy. We will remain vigilant. We will stand in the gap. We will nurture a generation that is healthy in mind, body, will, and emotion. Their generational wealth will include the wealth of Scripture!

Women of God, take your rightful place in your homes and protect these kids. This is a war for the soul of our nation, and that soul is in the heartbeat of our children. *Amen.*

ENTRY

Our lived reality is not God's reality. The all-knowing teenage perspective is not true; it is self-centered. The world perspective is broken. Many of us have made *lies* our *refuge.* Many of us have built on broken foundations (Psalm 11:3).

Women of God, it is time to build and restore.

We are called to be the *repairers of the breach* for our families (Isaiah 58). It is time to fast and pray. Fasting destroys generational, written, and time-released curses and turns them into blessings. Fasting exposes and destroys all plots and plans of the enemy. When we fast and pray, we are able to hear God's instructions clearly. God wants to make covenant (a forever agreement) with us. The role of this covenant is to protect us from the curses of the enemy. The devil is trying and will continue to attempt to destroy this covenant; a broken covenant with God allows curses to come in. The role of a curse is to allow evil spirits in our lives. *No more!* You are called to be the *restorer of streets to dwell in* (Isaiah 58:12). Our homes, our children, and our communities will be repaired and restored in Jesus' name.

Lord, help us to know the difference between a holy and unholy covenant. Help us to hear Your voice clearly and understand that Your covenants are explained in detail and in truth. There is no confusion about what we come into agreement with You, Jesus.

Lord, help us to recognize, rebuke, and reject the deception that the devil tries to trick us into coming into agreement with. Close every open door to every familiar spirit. Block every dream, every unconscious decision, and idle thought that the enemy might try to use to sign agreement with him and break covenant with You, Lord. We plead the blood of Jesus over the mind, will, emotion, and intellect of ourselves, our children, and our family members.

We love You, Lord, and we love all your rules, commandments, and principles laid out for us in the Word. May we hide them in our hearts that we may not sin against You (Psalm 119:11).

Lord, may You get all the glory out of our

> *lives. Restore our foundations. Give us a spirit of power, love, and a sound mind*
>
> (2 Timothy 1:7).
>
> *Amen.*

ENTRY

Things are put in our way to overcome them. Take *dominion*, women of God! Allow God to change everything to fulfill His will. *Amen.*

ENTRY

We need to know and appreciate the laws of the Bible. To *know* the answer is to reply to a legal charge. The devil is accusing us, our children, and our family day and night (Revelation 12:10). We must go to the court of heaven, where the Comforter, the Holy Spirit, is the counsel of defense. We cannot lose! *Amen.*

> "... 'Call to me and I will answer you. I'll tell you marvelous and wondrous things that you could not figure out on your own.'"
>
> (Jeremiah 33:3 MSG)

ENTRY

God has a natural order. He made man and woman to recreate and share the good news of His Son, Jesus Christ. This is why marriage and family are so important to a society. They bring generational blessings and wealth. However, if the devil can convince a child, woman, or man that they are gay, lesbian, transexual, etc., the destruction of that natural order comes in, wiping out entire families, bloodlines, and generations of people who will not exist for God's glory.

We must be consistent in our prayer lives, women of God! We

must not allow this to happen—not on our watch! Cover your home, your family, and your children in prayer. Plead the blood of Jesus over your bloodline and over generations to come. Speak life! *Life is a spirit!* May the Spirit of God hover over your home and God's will be fulfilled on the earth. God's Kingdom come. His will be done on earth as it is in heaven (Mathew 6:10). *Amen.*

ENTRY

Have you noticed any patterns in your parenting? I definitely have:

1. I remember while being pregnant with my son, I was getting ready to board a plane, and I just kept crying, bawling, ugly crying out of control. Many years later, I was at another airport with my son as he prepared to fly out to go live with his father for his final year of high school. And once again, I was bawling my eyes out.

2. I remember when my son was a toddler, I arranged for him to live with my parents for a few weeks. I was still in the military and struggling with my failing marriage. The pressures combined with just giving birth to my daughter were overwhelming. I was not able to give her the attention she deserved and needed, and I just needed time to bond with her. Many years later, I had let my teenage son go live with his father because I was once again struggling with raising him alone as he got to the point where he needed his father, and I needed to re-focus and re-establish my relationship with my daughter.

3. I remember I was hanging up my picture frame that held photos of all twelve years of my son's school pictures, and the glass had cracked, but it did not shatter, and I was able to salvage it with glass glue. It reminds me to this day that even though my relationship with my son cracked over the years, it did not break completely or shatter, and it is still held together with the love of Christ.

I often asked God, "What does all of this mean?" And He finally spoke and had me look up Luke 2:23 (NKJV), which states:

> "... ('Every male who opens the womb
> shall be called holy to the Lord')."

God was constantly reminding me that my son, our children, are not our own; they belong to the Lord. We need to give them back to their heavenly Father and allow God to have His will in their lives, even when we do not understand it, and even though it hurts. Each child has an ordination, a purpose, and are called to serve the Lord. It is our responsibility, our ordination, as parents to lead them, guide them, and instill the Word of God into them so that they are fully equipped to do so. Are we always going to get it right? No, absolutely not. I raise both hand and admit I made many mistakes. That is what the crack in the glass of the picture frame represented. I was parenting from my wounds. But even in the midst of all the trial and error, I always understood how important my role was as a parent, as a mother, and tried my very best in what I knew to get it right. And the grace and mercy of God was the glue that held it all together.

My son is called holy to the Lord. He will fulfill the purpose and calling on his life. He will live and *not* die! The enemy has been consistently coming after his anointing, but those attempts are both null and void because my son has a praying mother. A warrior in the Spirit. And I fight for mine!

My daughter is covered by God. She will fulfill the purpose and destiny placed on her. The enemy tried to convince me to abort her, tried to sow seeds of resentment toward her for coming at a time I was not ready. But those attempts and lies have been rebuked, uprooted, and cast down. My daughter has been one of the greatest blessings to me and those around her. Her very life has saved mine in so many ways—physically, mentally, and spiritually. She is a light that no darkness will ever cover. She will live and *not* die! *Amen.*

Women of God, there is an attack on our male children in this nation. The *Pharaoh* and *Herod* spirits are on the rise to murder our firstborns physically, mentally, and spiritually. There is an attack on their masculinity—the very thing God called holy. Many of us have carried a *Moses* in our womb—the *deliverer* of our bloodlines. Many of us have carried a *Joseph* in our womb—the *provider* of generational wealth. Many of us have carried a *Samson* in our womb—the *protector* of our present and future generations. The list goes on. Do not let the enemy confuse and trick you to become the Pharaoh or the Herod who murders your own firstborn in the womb, the very child that God called blessed and holy.

Women of God, there is an attack on our female children also. The *Jezebel* and *marine/mermaid* spirits are after our daughters. Their identities are being stolen and masked by perpetrators who devalue their worth. They are being encouraged and praised for turning into whores of Babylon! There is an attack on their femininity—the very thing that God calls strength and beauty (Proverbs 31). Many of us have carried an *Esther* in our womb—the *defenders* of our family and communities. Many of us have carried a *Deborah* in our womb—the *hearers* and *voice* of God to the nations. Many of us have carried a *Jael* in our womb—the *opportunist* and *warrior* in the Spirit. Do not let the enemy distract you from delivering and giving birth to whom God has called His *daughter*.

And, if you have, *repent*, mourn for that loss, and plead the blood of Jesus to cover that baby's shed blood that cries against you. *Renounce* that child sacrifice and tear down that altar to Molech. *Replace* that unholy covenant with a holy covenant with God.

> *Father today, I renew my covenant with You.*
> *I make You Lord over my life. The breach has*
> *been repaired. I plead the blood of Jesus over it.*
> *I come back in covenant with you. Amen.*

Our children mean so much to God that He instructed even us to become more like a child to get into the Kingdom of heaven (Matthew 18). And not only that, but there are specific instructions for those who do not love, respect, or protect His children at all:

> *"But if you cause one of these little ones who*
> *trusts in me to fall into sin, it would be better for*
> *you to have a large millstone tied around your*
> *neck and be drowned in the depths of the sea."*

(Matthew 18:6 NLT)

God does not play about His children, and we should not either. We need to heal from our wounds, repent from our sins, live *holy* and *righteous* before the Lord, stay praying and fasting, and remember that our children belong to God.

Let's not get caught up in our greatness, but in the greatness of God. Let's not be the hindrance from our children getting to Jesus, but the accelerator and facilitator for them to run into His arms. Let's be blessed and healed in Jesus' name so that our children can reap the blessings of salvation, restoration, and promise. *Amen.*

> *"But Jesus said, 'Let the little children come to me and do not hinder them, for to such belongs the kingdom of heaven.'"*
>
> (Matthew 19:14 ESV)

Closing Thought and Prayer

I had a vision one night:
A pathway leading to a dark bare tree. And an unformed substance hovering over it and holding it in its hands like claws, like a crystal ball.

That bare tree is you sitting in the dark, helpless, unprotected, out of the will of God, hurt, and wounded.

That unformed substance hovering over it is the spiritual world, the dark forces, and the principalities that have you bound in their powers because of your vulnerable state. They have legal right to you, have sucked you dry, devoured your leaves, stripped you bare and naked, and left you to die. Not only that, but they also monitor you to make sure you stay in that state, defeated, broken, worn out, and hopeless.

Matthew 13:22 (NKJV) says, *"Now he who received seed among the thorns is he who hears the word, and the cares of this world and the deceitfulness of riches choke the word, and he becomes unfruitful."*

The reason why so many of us have ended up in this state—unfruitful, bare, wounded—is because we have no *Word* in us. We do not know how to fight, how to break unholy covenants, or understand the power and authority given to us.

"Whose minds the god of this age has blinded, who do not believe lest the light of the gospel of the glory of Christ, who is the image of God, should shine on them." (2 Corinthians 4:4 NKJV)

We have been *blinded* purposefully, distracted intentionally, and negatively influenced deliberately to choke out and cancel out any Word of God that may help us to heal, to grow, and to live the abundant life that God has in store for us. That has and always will be the attack on the enemy. He may have perfected this skill since the beginning of time, but nothing's new because he is *not* a *Creator*.

The devil is a fierce manipulator through three simple tactics: the lust of the flesh, the lust of the eye, and the pride of life. That's it. That's all he's got. But we fall for it every time. Why? Because we do not know the Word of God. We must know and understand the laws of God, the promises of God, and the principles and precepts of the Word of God. This is our life source! Remaining in a state of ignorance could mean life or death, women of God! This could mean life or death for our children, for our children's children, to the third and fourth generation of our entire bloodline. We have to know and believe that we shall live and not die! Our children will live and not die! The veil has been torn so that the light of the gospel will shine through for those who are perishing. Pray that God shines through just enough light for you to see the truth. To see the only way. To see the *life*! *Amen.*

May you allow the light of Christ Jesus to:
- ❖ overcome your darkness
- ❖ expose your secret, hidden things
- ❖ show you the *way*
- ❖ give you hope
- ❖ give you peace
- ❖ bring you and your family your salvation

❖ bring healing to you and your bloodline

May you embrace God's illumination that comes through the Word of God. Get yourself out of the way. Get back into the Word, women of God! Psalm 119:105 (NKJV) says *"Your Word is a lamp to my feet And a light to my path."*

Lord, we come to You humbly. We cast off our crowns and lay down our scepters. Any other god we had before You we tear down and repent.

As Job 42:5-6 says, "I have heard of You by the hearing of the ear, But now my eyes see You. Therefore I abhor myself, And repent in dust and ashes."

Lord, please remove anything that is not of You out of me. I want to be holy as You are holy. Burn it out of me. I hate this flesh! I submit it to Your will, God. More of You and none of me. Heal me from my wounds, my hurts, and my pains. Forgive me for bleeding over my children. Help them heal.

I plead the blood of Jesus over myself, my children, and my future generation. For by Your stripes, we are healed. Thank You for insight. Thank You for our restoration. Thank You for Your grace and mercy. I love You, Lord. I come into covenant with You and You alone.

Holy Spirit, lead me and guide me in all truth. Root me and plant me by the rivers of living water that flow from the sanctuary of heaven, so that I may pour out life to those around me.

Rivers of Living Water. Cover me, cover my children, cover my family. May our foundations be firm on You.

Your Kingdom come.
Your will be done.
On earth as it is in heaven.
Hallelujah and amen.

Now, women of God, I have lived it. This is my personal testimony, just one of my "lived" realities. It is time to share yours. The Bible says that we can overcome the enemy by the word of our testimony (Revelation 12:11). That is how powerful our stories can be. Do not let the enemy trick you into thinking you have nothing great or grand to share, or that no one would ever care what you have to say. Lies! Who created you and said you were wonderfully made? God did! Who gave you life and purpose? God did! So listen to God!

Now go! Much work is to be done!

My dear SISTER:

Strong
Inspiration
So
That
Everyone around her
Reflects her beauty
(1 Timothy 2:9-10; 1 Peter 3:3-4)

> *"I would have lost heart, unless I had believed That I would see the goodness of the Lord In the land of the living. Wait on the Lord; Be of good courage, And He shall strengthen your heart, Wait, I say, on the Lord!"*
>
> (Psalm 27:13-14 NKJV)

The command from God is to wait on Him. And in your waiting, seek first the Kingdom of heaven and all its righteousness. In your waiting, get His Word in you. In your waiting, learn how to truly fast and pray. In your waiting, cry out to God in a posture of humbleness and repentance. In your waiting, *heal*, be renewed and made whole.

And may the perfect *Shalom* (peace) of God abide in you and your family from this day and forever more. *Amen.*

Always,
Your SISTER, Anna~

"'Many daughters have done well, but you excel them all.' Charm is deceitful and beauty is passing, But a woman who fears the Lord, she shall be praised."

(Proverbs 31:29-30 NKJV)

About the Author

Anna currently lives in North Carolina. She has two children, Jayden and Janiah. She has always had a passion for helping women through difficult situations in life one-on-one, in groups, and in speaking events. From someone who has personally gone through abortions, miscarriage, separation and divorce, anxiety, depression, emotional and sexual abuse, and single parenting pains, writing has been a way for her to process her thoughts.

She has decided to gather and share her life experiences, her cries, and her prayers with you in hopes that you can be encouraged, especially if you can relate. In a world where many sadly cannot define what a woman is anymore, Anna understands what it is to be a *woman*, the journey of *womanhood*, and the importance of sharing her life journey with others. A woman's testimony is unique and powerful, and it can truly make an impact on other women to hear that they are not the only ones in the world going through their situations. It can give hope in what one may have thought was a hopeless situation. And that hope can continue on to many generations.

My dear sisters, may this series bless your dry, thirsty souls, and bring healing to your land. In Jesus' name. *Amen.*

4cheartseries@gmail.com

Read More

I pray that my book series helps and encourages you in your emotional and spiritual walk throughout this thing called life. May you be blessed, healed, and made whole in Jesus' name. Amen.

Book 1: *Words for Seasons: Journal Entries of My Life Story*
Link: https://www.amazon.com/Heart-Thirsty-Seasons-Journal-Entries-ebook/dp/B098FBCYF4?ref_=ast_author_dp

Book 2: *My Journal Journey into Womanhood*
Link: https://www.amazon.com/Heart-Thirsty-Journal-Journey-Womanhood-ebook/dp/B0BBYSXNVT/ref=tmm_kin_swatch_0?_encoding=UTF8&qid=&sr=

www.ingramcontent.com/pod-product-compliance
Lightning Source LLC
Chambersburg PA
CBHW071033080526
44587CB00015B/2591